CORDAY

C O R D A Y

BY
MICHAEL MOTT

Walton Beacham Editions
Beacham Publishing

ISBN   0-933833-15-6

Printed in the USA

First Printing, November 1986

Books by Michael Mott

POETRY

THE COST OF LIVING (1957)
THE TALES OF IDIOTS and NEW EXILE (1957)
A BOOK OF PICTURES (1962)
ABSENCE OF UNICORNS, PRESENCE OF LIONS (1976)
COUNTING THE GRASSES (1980)

NOVELS

THE NOTEBOOKS OF SUSAN BERRY (1963)
HELMET AND WASPS (1966)
MASTER ENTRICK, juvenile (1966)
THE BLIND CROSS, juvenile (1969)

BIOGRAPHY

THE SEVEN MOUNTAINS OF THOMAS MERTON (1984)

In the poem . . .

the PLACE is Cambridge, Massachusetts, during the Bust and Student Strike at Harvard, April 8 through April 18, 1969. It is also Paris during the Terror.

CORDAY is the historical Charlotte Corday (see the note at the end), also memories of a number of women, including an activist and poet, and an owl.

The Villain is the painter Jacques-Louis David. There is no hero.

A WINDY NIGHT, the streets to Harvard Yard
are shrill with claxtons, tense with bursts of static
and voices arguing out of empty squadcars.
I watch a cockroach make an ill-considered turn
draft letters in a Lee Street kitchen to a dead fanatic.

She leaves no news of her, no note. Is she in prison?
Hurt? Phones ring where no one waits, urgent
for answerers. I fill the kettle, switch on light
to summon table, chairs. It hardly matters
what song Spring's rumors sing tonight.

Thunder and lightning, wagons and the Wain
Bootes and the Maiden, Scales and the Fruitgarland.
Samson, not Atlas, has a hand in heaven.
I cross my Xes. Black vans pass by laden.
Tear gas spreads on the wind like leaven.

ENTER Corday, the aspect of an owl;
a bird with gloves roves on the shifting rim
wanders the cloudy whirlpool of the lamp.
Instinct of sorrow and a curse no less
than curdled Argos, all the night a flight.

Matchless assassin, in this hour we owe
truth to our tyrants, to all oppressors, truth—
the cracks the ceiling shows, the lurid graph
of mere appearance. Then pare off
each piteous plaster with a baker's knife.

Changed out of Ovid to a bird, the baker's wife
who mocked at Christ, Fantastic Madge
mobbed by the tyranny of human faces.
Peace to the images you cannot staunch
all corners packed with rats, shadows, *canaille* of God.

"MEN have no place in this," she says.
I nod, correct the English of her posters.
She goes to horror films, prefers
movies where women are humiliated.
I have no answer. "Give Us Back The Night!"

Obscurity. The shades of Cambridge darken.
Men have no place in this. I push the text
corrected now, across the table.
She yawns and shaves her legs
then takes the telephone into the bathroom

calls other lovers, comes naked
to the bed. Alarms as raw as sirens
unlock our arms. In the half dark
she makes us coffee, black and scalding.
Dawn on the cat tracked sills, the dead geraniums.

SUPPOSE a truce made between knife and fork
a peace patched up for Tweedles Dum and Dee
and on the guanoed ledges pigeons slept
soot settled on the street. In Buzzard's Bay
the foghorns faltered. In the Berkshires

the sheep stopped coughing, engines rose
still groaning into air and disappeared.
Lovers who lay apart ceased breathing.
A silence like an earthfall let them in.
Bats and opossums overlay their children.

Only the moon kept climbing in the glass
across a waste of white. One ravelled cobweb
trailed like an afterbirth, jerked from a pin.
And on the windowsill a fly upturned
spun until morning. Friction burnt it black.

SHE LEAVES the dishes draining in the moonlight
goes out into the night, the violent night
to hunt for love, or to attend a meeting –
coven or caucus – for the lure of roads . . .
a cat trapped in wisteria roots and howling.

Her mystery's in the moods, the last French novel
pamphlet or film. I'd never get it right
who watch the clocks, fear the old fear of forests
and river banks – the baker's daughter
alone under the dripping trees – not quite

alone. What horror in such dreaming
the dream I dream on other nights made real!
Stalker and fearer. So we argue
each with ourselves and claim the best for cause.
The worst cancels our smiles with claws.

GIVE me your password, glass: *"Non pasaran."*
A hag whose dirty mobcap blocks the moon whistles a tune
sucks in her cheeks and tries another verse, the curse
of beggars and a clinking can. *"Non pasaran."*
Tonight all the roads are ambushed and all passes blocked.

Bivouac of gypsies in a house of crystal.
The bearded horseman stretches on the sofa.
Black bottles, empty, roll across the parquet.
The moon in mirrors watches as a peasant child
tries on balldresses, listless and beguiled.

Lice in the folds of fans, fat moths in fur.
Fire gossips of the woods, then someone spits–
retort of flames, steel scraping on a scabbard.
I turn the picture to the wall. From down the hall
a drunkard missing steps whines "Mother," "Mother."

PLATO, who gave a soul to plants, would know
how almond blossom's incandescent in the moon.
Token of Spring in streets, our only tree
that's not a soot scarred plane, your petals glow
like alabaster to some hidden flame.

Make what you will of this in Normandy and Kent:
on Appalachian slopes or in Granada—
who have whole orchards need no single tree—
and of this only part, perhaps four twigs . . .
the rest's bent, blackened, still in winter.

These almonds never ripen into food for weddings.
They're used, still green, in children's summer feuds.
Ovid, who gave a voice to a neglected almond tree
might speak for you. To me, you're one more rumor
shedding through the dark glass your calm mandorla

LET down the spider to the foretold fall.
Corday, I say, a little madness is a wonderous thing:
too much, you lose yourself for ever.
Between a world of stone and one of air
you, or some part of you, sleepwalks and never

ceases to croon or sing like sailors raising chain
or weavers *waulking* out the wool on Skye.
We'd dream a skill in talking to a rope
whose tension is at times our only hope.
You step by such sure falls against the light

defined by space, knowing day by night.
Soft wings fill up the window. In a crush of wings
eyes animate the glass. Corday, I say
guilt's not the worst thing we can feel.
The dawn unseen. A sprinkler laying dust.

THE PADDY WAGONS back up to the Yard.
The Dean's goons hold the gates. "Pusey
Must Go! Must Go!" The nightsticks crack.
The ambulances fill. I watch the leak
glistening on privet leaves. Must go. Must go . . .

And she's not here. In prison? Dead?
Mechanical as clocks, the chant, *"Ira!"*
The Rights of Man to hunt our double down
our luckier double. Children of the rich
the Keystone Cops from every precinct come

converge on Cambridge, grown serious. The Spring
unwraps magnolia buds, crimson and white
on Arlington. A cold wind blows. Wisteria
gnarled as old hausers cracks the ornate iron.
Blood on her scarf, she greets me: "Fucking pigs!"

THE CHILD took up the missal, but remade
her features—a small moue—to mock the glass.
Glass is not mocked, no *commedia dell'arte*
only a rack for shadows. Tighten skin and lips.
Your vanity, Corday. No venal sin.

The questioner set chairs and cleared the table.
"Your friends?" he said. "Your friends? Your friends?"
And smiled, a jester, or unable to dissemble.
Hours passed. The agony was lost on glass.
What bores bores to the quick. It made a picture.

But there were always other pictures in the room.
Who chooses these we never need to know.
If bats were bells, perhaps you thought, and I
hung from my heels, what answer when he rings?
Corday, I say. We can't afford to lie.

BE constant, Charlotte. Everywhere we meet that other
who's angry with us, always half ashamed;
who spoils the harmony of every careless hour
creature and comforter, our enemy and friend;
whose power's persistent, if unnamed.

Grown too familiar for contempt, this hoarder
cranks up old images, has anecdotes, statistics
to prove that we were always awkward, sometimes sly.
Who holds the keys to drawers and haunts night laundries
should know when *not* to blush at a white lie.

A lackey soul who'd make a good Court Painter
or serve as spy for any claque that calls
has some discretion, knowing what's at stake.
Who cuts us down sounds the self-valet, maid
and leaves an empty glass, a view of walls.

SPRING nights, the riot of the young.
Bright lights all night in Academe
argue Apollonian orders of the day.
Three hundred years—shall even Harvard
burn! Black flames of ivy climb. "I'd

like to think the trees deliver us from
history, root and branch, in getting
the air clean of all the deeds of men.
My history lectures in the Grove are
cancelled. Drink. Drug. Reason has always

been a circular argument. It never argues
with Unreason. Given the premises . . . If
I were young again I'd never wear this gown."
Cop-out, both ways. Two cop cars, fore and aft,
talk to each other in the smoldering dawn.

ANOTHER June, when Dunce the Third was King
when all the Bucks and Beaus in Rotten Row
were gossiping of France, and how the Frogs
deserved their dubbing; how one Austrian blow
one British frigate off Toulon, would end it.

Well, let them bleed awhile: *"extirpate Carthage!"*
They helped one lot of rebels in America;
now Liberty's sailed home. Lafayette, Mirabeau
can quizz it at first hand. England
knows better – hang five, and transport all the rest

in fetters . . . Demme, prettiest gel I ever saw! . . .
Scorn on Mobocracy. True Freedom – Common Law.
The poor content on Beer and Hollands.
Flogged if they're not. All Free-Born
Englishmen, God Bless 'Em . . . Martin, call the dogs.

WHAT laughing images were looted from the dead?
A picnic on Cape Cod where pourer pours
and something fills the glass and drains the face.
Two women sprawling on a tartan rug
white blouses full. Hands emphasize the place

where all the creases of their dresses run.
A certain sureness in their power to please
stays in the eyes. Smiling, they try
to keep their poise, unsquinting, in the sun
and fail. A shadow like a gnomon's falls between.

Thin even crouching, the fourth guest, unseen
flows, a wild zigzag, over cups and plates.
A dog looks up in time for the sharp click.
It is the dog's gaze now unmans the scene—
his sense suspended animation hides a trick.

A DRAGONFLY with four black flags for wings
hangs by its head, pulsating body free.
Too much good fortune makes the spider slow.
She keeps her larder neat with muslined hams.
This monster tears down walls and won't let go.

Not in, not out, it pulls the piece awry.
Drags down one corner almost to the sill.
Still waving semaphores of black distress
he stretches out his tail to wood, to glass.
Some predawn draft keeps pushing him away.

I search for scissors, hardly break my stare
but now the web hangs free, no dragonfly.
One filament careening on the air
and in the unaltered center, grown serene
turn by slow turn, the spider wraps the head.

WHAT flatters Judith with the trophied head?
Moonlight evades the question, and the painter's dead.
But any child who knew their nursery rhymes
might find the answer easy, and their innocence—
which is no fairytale—could chill the blood.

Ambiguous legends pass for what's unsaid.
What Holofernes is, let Ph.D.s
who find nine hundred names for irony
explain, and all their theses lie unread—
Evoke no image of the mountain slope

where Pentheus waited. Spies who know their trade
are shy of other spies, of animals, and children.
They speak with graver men who know the world, and women
who never look in glass too far. Who talk too much.
A strange, truncated, story maybe, but the story's ended.

CUT out the eyes and make the tears from glue.
False priests have addled all confession.
A tale of Bruegel's blindmen, Goya's two
battering each other further into mud—
I set four *"Frére Jacques"* for each omission.

They say Goldoni had his training as a torturer—
his hundred comedies: The Human Heart Laid Bare.
How picturesque to find a moral here
among the shadows of a print by Piranesi
and smudge by smudge make out the features flayed.

Charlotte, I say, white clover made your mask
when owls were born in Wales, when sorcerers' wives
cut down the creamy barley with curved knives—
a Milky Way, frost flowers on glass, the Danaides
whose tasks with water were a kind of absolution.

OWL calls to owl across the night.
Scherzi di Fantasia. The forest family
of satyrs makes its camp beside the lake.
Among the tombs and broken urns and skulls
they nurse their children, play with curling snakes.

Under a brushstroke pine—half girl, half woman—
one stares into the starfilled water.
No wind chills her small breasts or stirs
her contemplation by a single ripple.
Calm to the wanderer, content of places.

These graceful refugees in others ruins—
a world inherited by waterfowl and owls and fauns—
and one upon the crossroads of two lives
within herself, the breaking dawn of love
love for her body's power, that vast disturbance.

A MOTH crawls sideways, shakes uncertain wings
a glider caught in trees, curtain of beads
a smear of coaldust on the flagrant page.
Boats over water—and the lamp
steadies itself to see the miner down

steadies itself to see the diver drown.
Castles of coral and the cursive gold
runes of blue lead, a runaway of knots.
In groins one cyclops stares with grotto eye.
Pressure of wind or water on the glass.

Darkness explores the dark, pullies and stays
rumor the wings. Miner or diver gone
across a sill, by cage, by keel, by blade.
The toggles slip like spawn, a line of beads
running the tide, draws to the lodestone shore.

CHARLOTTE, I say a child could pluck your wings.
A peasant nail your maiden veils to a barn door.
Blood becomes any rust. The satyr of the wood
is closer to mankind than many men.
Lemurs have died for love for all I know.

I see a world of windows through the glass.
What was let out is crying to be let in.
What flew before is now a fall of ash.
Give me your claws to write our names on glass.
Give me your hair to hang a web in glass.

Our prisons never break. The tyrant child
begs back his bones. This night alone will fade
like any other. Only the coupled prey
escape an edict where the talons clash.
The scream of fingers on a field of glass.

INCESTUOUS wars, infanticide of pride:
fathers who kill their sons by proxy, mothers
who bait the trap the rabid Mother State
sets for pale sisters of the bullying brothers–
honor and war and wailing and betrayal.

What saved the play, what conjured wind
into limp sails, moved the unmovable with awe
claims at each nursery crib its pound of fable–
gods of the hearth and all of Hecate's stable
mother grown stern, the kindly, baffled father.

Masking the glass incense of Brumaire lingers.
Three raps I give the floor, the curtain cringes
but there's no play, granddaughter of Corneille
of ancestors or owls. Instinct, not reason
allots the sacrificial parts–mice, mice, and fingers, fingers.

DUTY and Love, Corneille—
Duty of Love, and Love of Duty—
these two go shouting down the Chorus
until they bore us. Tell me there's freedom
left in love, to love, to leave still loving.

Enough. Duty's the death of love and
loneliness of the long marriage. Fickle
in freedom, we keep the right to change
deceive, and pay for our deceipt—
so duty win, that is the term of freedom.

In love—who knows? Who ever knows
where love will lead?—self-death, self-doubt . . .
The bugles calling from the far caserma
and Carmen near. Touch is no treason.
The dream of reason fades. Warm-blooded monsters.

AMBIGUOUS talk tonight. Across the tundra
a gray moss grows on craniums of stone
the arctic lichen in alchemic riot
spills jewelled colors in a blackened pot.
Wind tampers here with wards of locks.

And she confides her dreams of torturers
men masked as birds, masked cardinals
who peck her flesh. She pets the cat.
And I say nothing. While the wind
crosses the arctic plains, cold, cold

that jabbers here, jabbers with iron tongues
insinuate secrets as she smiles. "It's nothing,"
she says. "It shows no scars." She laughs.
"I've fantasies far worse . . ." The cat holds
me with such a gaze I scrape my chair, rise, go.

"REMEMBER me!"—As well remember rain
or Agamemnon and the baths where he was slain.
Crossing the carpet, wary of the hole
I pull the carpet after to the door—
block out the draft!

Ignore an Alexander in an Indian pool.
That dust's not settled yet. The wind
breaks out of Asia rolling dross
of chestnuts. As a rule
I turn the lock.

Another night. Across the marvelous glass
the raindrops run. They pass
unreachable. I think of Pliny's carp
rising to taste the salt of living things.
Rain isn't that.

COME, whirling Dervishes and ragged bobbins
skate, caper on the moonlit glaze of glass;
play crack-the-whip and paperchase and tag;
or leapfrog one another where the gale
snaps on itself and howls between high walls.

Or stream, a million minnows, silver streaks
under the streetlights, down the caverned alleys
over the trashcans and green, glistening sacks
slumped on the sidewalk by the silver hydrant.
Flee through the fire escapes and chainlink fences

over the chimneystacks and watertanks.
Hover like starling packs, by masts, antennae—
then sweep, one golden horde, fall, settle
on iron, on stone, on any cap or cornice
on steps below the wind, at every ominous doorway.

NO certain wisdom, but a gaze of owls.
Like one who held the glass to Athens in the plague
and wrote no history. Yet who left the rats
to fester with their fleas
under black Attic suns, and lived.

Such was the rack and ruin of the State.
Minerva's bird. What's Athens to an owl?
Brooding and mewing to the moon
another watched the dark ships sail for Syracuse
and never wondered who or what came back.

Your mask was tragic if we want it so—
utter indifference to all human fate.
Pisan, Venetian, Turk, or Greek—
two obols on the lids. And under this
in owl emptiness what dark abyss?

SOME cop thrusts her against a fence
and twists her shoulder. "No Nukes!"
I rub in ointment, note the long
fall of her body almost without passion.
What strange companions. Close the drapes.

It is her nakedness, so vulnerable
I'd close her in my hands, keep safe
all that I almost love. And yet the flesh
is for the mending. Drill the mind
to protest now against possession

for I touch surface, not the spirit
that tolerates my hands. Ambiguous friendship
warms both our bodies in unquestioned kin.
The iron rain still falls on every chainlink—
rusting, rusting. We each survive apart.

SLOW, burning, beauty—
the driftwood tea of far Cathay—
I hold her features and pretend
to look away
to look away.

Another afternoon is over.
In the Cambridge dusk
Taprobana's ants have carried off
gold grains of day
gold grains of day.

Some little Empress of the Chan
who took to bed the bearlike horseman—
the sweat of mares, pink foam of May.
No more to say.
No more to say.

CHARLOTTE, expect the unexpected. When you call
be sure the monster's playing with his children.
He'll have a pleasantly distracted wife who knits.
A maid lays table. "Will you stay for supper?"—
who stand so awkwardly, keeping your coat, your muff.

But will not exit. It's as if you knew now
fate overloads the stage for such austere occasions
making all plots like yours unworkable as fiction
that may turn fact. Even had you anticipated
that Horror played such scenes behind the scenes

would you have guessed, when it was over
that you would risk a moment staring back on glass?
In love, where more than one's in danger of being caught
your double, or some woman too much like your double
holds in her lap the bare and bloodied feet.

THE CHAIRBACK casting bars across the table
brings names of prisons into our debate.
Madame Richard, the kindly turnkey at Conciergerie
shows off a hank of chestnut hair. Such keepsakes
are freely given, too, at Saint Pelagia, La Force

where Rousseau's bust surmounts the classic altar
of Liberty—at Bicêtre, and L'Abbaye . . .
A Feast of Reason and September's dead:
pickpockets, prostitutes, artistocrats
mingled in bloodstains that outstay the rain
darkened to ordure, rank *Egalité* of death.

Charlotte, I think I know a tale more terrible than this
when spies became the heroes of an age:
when tyrants ran the trains on time to fill the graves . . .
There is a double game in shame that gloats on shame.
I stare on glass, will not compete in crimes.

LOOK for more perfect men, Lenin, St. Just—
poor workman clay will fail Promethean lust.
Cold neo-classic dreams of self-denying grandeur
blue bruise the raw, the ever-falling flesh.
Give to the gods Horatius, not our friend.

Our friend, who crawls with lice and stinks of drink
whose backstreet lecheries are little news
sends shots from cigarettes into all corners
and will betray us, but betray us less
than cold philosophers: Augustine, Calvin, Marx.

Tonight, the soft snow falls on Cambridge—
ideal landscape, flakes that blacken, soot
or smudge, black ice . . . But for the moment
the windows light the town where every surface
speaks of a new beginning, some unlikely chance.

THESE start the dance, slow saraband of wings.
Poor faces without masks, poor faces
naked to light, a play of planes and holes
filled with fine gauze, pupilled by insects
you rise and slump for air, poor bobbins.

Brooms, mops, coats, hats, come, take your places!
Storm all the cupboards, free the boots and shoes.
The winter ball begins, the music's thin
but coming nearer: flagpoles, halyards, wires
drumming of plumbing, looser panes of glass.

Gavotte and trot, whole families of newspaper
scarves hornpiping from drawers, fans clapping.
Trunks burst their hinges. Whooping, out they spill,
plumed, painted for the wardance, each one shrills:
"Republicans! Now is the time of Things!"

SOMETHING there is makes negatives of this.
Tonight a woman floats against the glass suckling a child
whose glistening skull is blue, whose eyes are closed.
I cannot see her own eyes till she turns
slow saraband—pinpricks of white.

I cannot say her face has an expression.
The wind blows her long skirts against the panes.
They bump, pause, bump. A length of rope
sashes that flow straight in before a storm
would make that sound, but these are soft, insistent.

And now I hear the child's lips at the breast.
Gutteral. It buts and gnaws, draws deep.
A thread of black milk trickles to the chin.
I raise the lampshade. In the shock of light
something's still there—a little dome, bone blue.

WHAT lullaby?–A tale of ink-black ivy
a white web and the drops too dark for pearls.
Moonlight throws smaller squares across the table.
The buttons on my cuff untune the fork
then the fork falls.

Sleep's dusty powders: henbane, opium, belladonna—
soft chemistry of shifting grains.
Someone stamps up the staircase from the cellar.
I count the stairs and landing out before
he tries the door.

However late, I'd burn my papers into feathers,
erase your name. Instead, I watch a globe
assume each pattern in the patterned room.
He pounds and goes. Turn back to glass. From walls
small plaster falls.

THE STREETLIGHT smolders, and what drunkard's song
brings Dublin nearer as the words ring clear?
Each brick in walls and every pavingstone
takes up the notes, the snaredrum sound of feet.
Something stirs in the glass. Two echoes meet

and blend. But what they make together makes no sense.
Was it lost Creusa, or the cocklefisher's daughter?
Was it in Baggot Street, or Troy deserted
I heard the poor corpse sing "ALIVE-O" through the city?
There was a strolling player once who sung that ditty

with such a resonance the Argives hid their eyes.
As one man, they declared they'd never been *near* Troy
denied they knew the cockler's daughter. As for Helen
she'd always been a ghost. Ask Menelaus.
Grown maudlin drunk, they keened the chorus: "Oh, ALIVE-OOOO!"

SMOKE from the tripod, watches of the night.
A dream of Greece before the goat was king . . .
Before a gorgon stare turned all the groves to stone
and set a seal of glass on pool and spring—
O, Arethusa, all's to underworld!

Thickets of Thessaly, slow barcaroles of planes.
What moves below—above me—in the night?
Murmers of water and the muscled flood.
What sets the housegods jangling in their fright
rumbles the panes, and stirs dark birds to flight?

A figure trailing rags like riverweeds
turns into Lee Street, curses as he reels
at bruising stones, the clamor of the birds:
"I'm dead, not drunk, you damned Eumenides!"
Then sprawls. Black water licks his heels.

STARS in the glass and shadows on the wall:
what greater Fortune's drawn, what Gnomonics?
What Babylonian lore, what casts of darkness?
Pure chance, perhaps, that prompted Fabre's spiders
that shapes the hive and haunts wood-boring bees—

whose art's an instinct. And what greater fortune
than to know nothing of the pattern of the cast
when what we build in some sure trance of building
exists already somewhere in the air as fact?
And can be broken, left unfinished, but not spoilt

by any striving? Is it all envy then, and imitation
to let our dreams or our machines take over from us
the unsure, clumsy dance, the half-charade of reason?
I'll make my art my own and then disown it.
Stars in the glass and shadows on the wall.

WHITE nights, across the glass the ravenous spider
checks out her moonlit traps, finds each one empty—
nothing hunched on its knees like a bent pin.
Only an open field, the smudged, fast filling tracks
a web on a round scar, an odd fir beckoning back . . .

Far is too far, test out the lines, the Grand Design.
Snow stalks the angry hunger in your head.
I light a lamp to guide you in the night
blinding your eyes and blackening where you tread—
River run backwards. Weaver, find your thread.

Maps of the mind, lost keys to labyrinths
star charts without the stars. At unknown urging
pilot- and compass-less, white winter nights
caught in a web of beams, bemused, past fear
we drift in snow toward calm wastes of snow.

CORDAY, I read Bakunin, then Camus
who scarcely mentions you
for numerous Russian
babushkas with their bombs.
Sweet Terrorist, *The Rebel*

needs you more surely than
its czars exploded, its Nina
Nihilists. Life for a life.
"If we had known what she had
planned, we would have pointed

to Robespierre first—Marat
was a dead rat already—or
Danton." Your tame Girondists
were marked already for the Maiden.
Corday, what's lost but life?

CHARLOTTE, for virtuous Romans Roman holidays.
Bathos, not tragedy. If those not starved are bored
be sure their jeers and their applause are one—
ambiguous praise, ambiguous desecration.
You weave a scarlet thread into their gray.

These are the fateless ones, who, tier by tier—
those in the sun, those in the shadow—make
their gladiators heroes, stoic slaves
mock Hector, mock Achilles, test vicarious ground
blood, blood; sand, sand—so citizens can sleep

in stew and suburb. Served your heart or head
they'll snore their satisfaction, dream a double life.
Tonight one Saturnalia ends, another starts.
A woman with a knife sleepwalking walks
in private rooms made fast against the storm.

WHO play at Fate, these terrorists of the mind
Cassandras of the cocktail party, pose no threat.
Their message is a war within, uncivil, civil.
The world they walk in has no walls but flesh.
Pale solipsists. Troy might be standing yet.

Marat might play with duck flotillas in his bath
and these be by to canvas for a cause
that is themselves, writ in a global hate.
No one will do their hair to show the snakes.
No one will teach them curses that can kill.

They have their maids. They winter in the sun.
They wax too hot to play the lesser part
of strange sleepwalkers waking to a dream
of justice, that will use them, throw them off—
nothing to conjure with, except a name.

THAT smaller moon, the eggcase of the spider
hangs by one thread beneath her spread of legs.
What clutched it in a setting like a jeweler's claws
grew limp in death, then locked again on air.
Unsheltered now, the sphere spins on the wind.

But will not flounder while the time fuse burns
primed by a mother's death, a father's murder.
Cronus ungendered, seed untimely ripped
from any pod. Chronology that breeds
from nameless crimes more time for nameless crimes—

more multitudes, whose progress, moral, is
more multitudes, frenzy for filling numbers, aim
so awesome in its mad simplicity, no future seems
sufficient room to test the potency of spiders.
The dead moon's borrowed light, white swollen carapace.

SAY that I feast with friends. The glass glows red.
Bedlam in streets and starlings in the sky.
Nothing more normal than the firetrucks' screams:
ladders and nightgowned angels, nests of snakes—
and all the boxes filled, the houselights high.

Pity poor Harlequin, a patchwork on a wire
saved by the net—pale Columbine . . . All saved
all safe, all shaken. Neighbors all grown kind.
The Capulets consort with Montagues, spies with spies.
Wailing and empty, the last ambulance retires.

Hardly an interval before the floodlit street
is shrill with whistles. Shots. The running feet
stop at the corner. Some glass object breaks.
The ambulance comes back. I wash up forks and knives.
Go back to work. My papers smell of smoke.

SURPRISED by bullets at the wall
he stands confused and looking back
as if someone had called to him.
Surprised by bullets at the wall
he stands confused and looking back.

Some sound still rumbles in the glass.
He gazes up and sees my light.
One in, one out, across the night.
Some sound still rumbles in the glass.
Our glances meet. He starts to laugh.

Our glances meet. He starts to laugh.
The seconds pass. The seconds pass.
So slowly nothing seems amiss
still grinning up, he starts to fall
surprised by bullets at the wall.

CAVEAT CANIS! Where the Dog Star rages
our only news is boredom and the heat.
Smokers, sleepwalking, pass by other windows.
A hound's still panting on the stoop.
At two a.m., can't bark, can't eat.

A single squadcar loiters at the corner.
Its red eye roves more indolent than angry
over the grilles and boarding of the stores.
The bassman in some otherwise lost group
keeps up the beat.

The lightbulb rickets, then goes out.
My papers curl. They sound like feet
slipping on sand. Something leaks in
around the drapes—from distant abattoires, perhaps—
a taint of meat.

CABIN of glass, all round the rank Sargasso.
Stink of the day's sun in decaying weeds.
Where can we travel, old Odysseus, sailor
through cabbages and crates and melon shells?
What landfall from the gangrened seas?

Say that Zipango was a fortnight's crawl
the Blessed Isles only a week away
through mangrove traps and scalding manchineel –
or Chana with its rats as large as dogs
or Pentexoire, more fabulous than Cathay –

and we not reach them. No, nor wallow home.
Circe was here who turned the whaletrack black.
They'll say we wrecked our galleon on a reef
to spite the owners, or sail now as pirates
sweeping the seas. Grow rotten in this wrack.

THERE was a monkey band played Mozart.
These porcelain figures one could break
with breath made every note sound so etherial
dolphins might weep. So Orpheus sang of death
to creatures, and the creature world replies.
This is an artificial thing, man made

so love is, so is grief. Eurydice, come back
to listen. Daphne in her laurel. So all
ideals are made with hands, with thought.
Creature to creature. Charm is only spell.
Circe, relent, cast back the swine to men

or let them sing swinesong as fine as this.
Sirens are seabirds. Only tune your lyre
one octave lower and you hear the sea.
The earth has voices only some beasts hear:
man, woman, and the leaves, the leaves.

I ONLY see the hands that smooth the sheet.
Another hour, an elbow and two breasts.
Someone strikes someone. Someone screams.
A girl falls backwards, naked, on the bed.
Curls instantly upon herself. The light goes out.

A Punch and Judy Show. A summer night
in parks that Fragonard might paint—
trees silver fawn and roses red as blood.
I stand and look across the moonlit street
ready to meet the sounds I think I fear.

When nothing further comes, the calm seems worse.
"Stop beating her!" I shout. "STOP BEATING HER!"
I scramble details down: the hands, two breasts, a scream.
I'm watching everything, I tell the glass. I'm witnessing.
And stare into that square of dark and start to weep.

NIGHT winds: Libs, Notus, Eurus, Apeliotes
blow the white dust of summer on the grass.
Neglected letters, books half read, pink notes
of phonecalls I've mislaid.
Make what excuse I will, August is over.

Blank calendars of paper or of stone
month of the locust, era of the rat;
what's left unanswered doesn't need an answer—
dry winds from Thebes
jostling the reeds that never made papyrus.

Take what's unwritten for a thought forgotten.
Against the wind Selene climbs so slowly
it might be the white snail that walked to heaven.
Strangers and parasites and friends
what's one less wedding guest? One grief unspoken?

DEAR Occupant: If you have written since we wrote
ignore this warning. But, if not, take note.
There is no evil anyone would wish you, but the time
is overdue, and you have left undone
what we had hoped for. Without more ado

look now to freeze in winter, live in dark
and eat raw meat. Expect in summer, heat—
no trash collections and no telephone
no television, and if that's not the worst
our curse arouses—give your taps a miss.

All this, if you can stand it, we will send
bailiffs, who'll leave you to bare wood and glass.
If, after that, you linger in your cave or flat, look to
eviction. This, we feel, will do. Respectfully
your friend, your humble servant, and sincere. Adieu.

YOU'VE made a martyr of Marat, Corday
and every dog expects apotheosis.
Each patriot swindler, cheat, and counterfeit
opens his doors to all the walking whores
in Paris, hoping just one has something

up her sleeve. Bakers explain their knives
were sharper than they knew . . . No, nothing
is ever easier than satire. But a hero's
not chosen by the gods without the moment.
To die like Seneca in a red bath . . .

be painted as the scapegoat, crucified
after a life so base! You gave them that.
Advantage. When they had nothing, nothing
but lists of dead, proscription . . . Sleep—
dream of French fields. I love you. Linger.

DREAM of French fields and river meadows
of days the hay was soft under your rake as hair
of Norman cider in great clumsy cups
of country marriages to drum and bagpipe
of streets so gray wisteria was a flaw.

Caen and its jackdaws. Nights and nightingales
in pocket gardens. Poverty that counts its sous
and weeps that we must eat. Old men still fighting
Marlborough. Women who know a reputation to a mote.
And mass on mornings when the fingers ache.

You big boned Norman girls with too much color
in the skin are marked in sallow Paris. Another wit
no courteous cringing. Something of a deep, hayloft
sleep in all you do. Least obvious assassin, awake
or dreaming. One blow, and downward, to the heart.

VISIT the Bedlam where four kings
deposed, and two dictators, play
at cards for blows. A former queen
screeches a violin. These rooms
become our minds revealed—these cells

of straw and ordure, messaged walls
calling on God, on Babadab, with
broken bars for days, and the loved thing
a ragdoll—all the shattered toys
of childhood, all reborn, and kinder

without eyes. No needles, pins—
no invitations. And our constant friends
specters who weep, but for themselves
without hypocrisy or cant. Each evening
a long cry through the wards like absolution.

EVENINGS draw gray anatomies on glass
lemurs no longer lithe, their bodies flayed
in places where the thin fur parts, their eyes so full
of madness where they stare they burn a trash
of callow pity like a burning glass.

Poor random Jacks, self-lust attacks
each at a turn. They shudder into sex
then scrub their eyes, their hair
or pelt the ghosts beside them into life—
a moment's uproar, then the vacant hours.

The keeper's dead who'd batter down the walls
to let unspeakable things out, to free
the beast to bay the beast. . . Against the glass—
cold touch of this is all the touch I fear—
I press my hand to match the palm I see.

CORDAY, I have no stamina to be a Cynic
but I'll not pity what's not worth a sneer.
Diogenes says—fast to starve desires
and if desires won't die, then try the rope—
who hadn't seen a hanged man rise to the occasion.

I'd rather be a huckster of my lust
exhibited, the wild man behind glass.
If I can't mask the satyr in the sage
I'd rather rage with monkeys in a pit.
Philosophy's a glutton for starvation.

All sex in sexlessness offends. My lust's a slave
to love, perhaps, but has a right to rave
at willful virgins and all sensual saints.
Ideals are lovely, but the flesh is warmer.
Owls go with owls. Diogenes saw whores.

"*NO hay asesino bueno en mi concepto,*" says Neruda—
"The righteous assassin does not exist," Corday.
And yet I wonder if you came to mind. Life for a life.
It's not the knife, I'd question, Corday, but the lies.
Well, there's an ending. I have lied for less

who make no claim to be a righteous killer
or patriot—the fields and hilltops that I cherish
make up no country, even in the mind. Who knows
if I might come to kill, and what I'd kill for—
I want no testing—friends, family; no mere abstraction. . .

That's what we all say. Come the day, who knows?
I study both my hands, wonder as Yeats did, if words
ideas of mine, sent out the death squads, bungling
boys, into the streets, the ambushes in hedgerows. . .
And nothing answered: all the casualties keep secrets.

CHARLOTTE, you'd say you acted and I talk.
Trapped in a web a fly has a small round to walk.
Lobotomized by lust the lemurs stare
across the glass, paralysis of air.
The bathcap on a broom waves from the barricade.

The moon sleepwaking pauses on a stair.
A broken platter in the kitchen sink
glares up through water. All I do is think.
You batter at my books, a jealous cat
would do as much and paw the pages flat

to settle upon any argument like that.
Your demilunes, *lunette*, a stop upon the stair
Aristo's birthmark, swallows cutting air.
Charlotte, you'd say you acted and I talk.
Trapped in a web a fly has a small round to walk.

PINK and white awning of the flower seller's—
there is cool music tinkling in this heat
fountains, white doves, retired from streets
the smell of kif, petroleum, chestnut dross.
We meet. Her hair is stale with sunlight.

I have odd pentimenti on my shirt.
In Grolier's windows all the books are melting—
white wax and words. Her voice. Her voice.
What's new? What's news?—All lovers leaving.
All Cambridge fleeing to the Cape.

We drink iced coffee and I take her picture
bored waiters for a background. All I hear
are traveller's tales of hippogriffs and rocs.
When Boston burns, she'll serve up salt for truth
some Dead Sea monster, desert birds, for proof.

THIS moment when the dawn glows orange
then block by block the windows change.
The sky and River Charles exchange
blue for a white. Pale grays arrange
themselves like feathers where the pigeons range.

It's not her lovers but her flaunting
drives me to bad decisions in the night.
Her ultimatums, all her taunting—
She'll love me only, only when it's right.
If I do this. . . If I'm the prey, she'll bite.

First jogger passing as I drink my tea.
The office workers hurry for the T
and Chinese gymnasts spill from M.I.T.
I risk her love, I'll risk her enmity—
in a completeness court complexity.

IT'S NOT an argument, love always wins
and yet we fight. She says:
"I'm happy in your lap, you know
when we have company, then
someone says 'Just what are you two doing?'"

Love always wins. She says:
"I'd like to go under your desk
when you have students, and you know."
And yet we fight, we fight.
It's not an argument, and yet . . .

She says: "I like to bump you
in the shower, and backwards, like,
you know." It's not an argument.
We fight, we fight, and yet
love always wins, and then, you know, you know.

THEY'D drive two rowan splinters through our hearts
if they knew what to bury, what to burn;
or build two cages, one of air, one glass;
or make a fable that we turned to stars–
and miss the point where any voices meet.

Substance, not shadow, was our rendez-vous
and these are masks I made, not quite disguises;
enough to pass the port, evade the spies
ward off the plague a while, confuse the Furies
and face the wind that picks away at posters.

What hunts us down will win no doubt, if winning
is the poor gumshoe scarlet on a file
of "Missing Persons"/"Found"/"No Longer Wanted".
Still far ahead of any grim pursuer
we part on Marlborough Street and let the rowan grow.

WHERE are you fleeing to, you auguring birds?
What *générale* resounded on deaf ears?
Or unseen headline flashed across the night?
What seawind mumured "*Catarrhine*"?
What subterranean music beats retreat

in us for Anthony, our power gone?
Treason in Egypt, in Alexandrian streets
Octavius' infiltrators; spies, collaborators...
Midnight–one hour too late, too late!
Bribes opened, orders closed the gates.

Citizens, friends, which watch are you–
Girondist? Fatalist? Jacobin?
Of the White Terror, Green, or Red?
What is the current password?–"Dead."
Then what's the living word?–"You heard."

CORPSES of kings, amateur locksmiths
the hobbyists and stamp collectors.
How little glory in a baffled booby
crammed in a bloody basket. How little
glory in the deed, a headless body.

How does it change the years of slow
starvation for the poor, the racketeering
schemes of Law, the silliness
of queens, the Church's deep corruption?
How does it dignify the bleating sheep

brought in so that the Court could play
at shepherds? What pettiness is this?
No dire revenge. No Brutus stabs his friend
hoping to stay the plunder of the State.
No Plutarch tells *this* tale. No wonder.

THIS, too, I saw. The Eagle and the Lamb.
A pack of bodies like old clothes in cupboards.
Children in arms brought to the Maiden.
Much courage. Much contempt . . . inhuman
or human?—all balances put out.

One lives—outlasts victims and judges—
to see strange things: the Queen of Reason
swived on an altar, Liberty a Tree—
too rooted in the dirt for me—Police
who serve each government for none, true

anarchists, whose solace is in lists
and three square meals and screams.
Their faces never change. Old tyrannies
at least were less efficient. All this
and more I mention in reports.

POLICEMEN and Painters will survive these times—
these policemen and *these* painters.
David, "one born to be a lackey"
said Robespierre, who policed
the paintings. David the fashion-catcher

spits on the dead Corday;
sketches the mobled Queen
going to slaughter; awaits a hero
the boss from Corsica; then candies
Psyche and Cupid.

Stendhal, who knew a soldier
when he saw one, laughs at
those Spartans fighting naked—
those Beaux Arts' nudes, flags
on their cocks for figleaves.

EDICTS of governments long out of power
peel on the walls and bleed in a black rain.
If some imperatives are wasted, some "DO NOT!"s
nothing much alters earlier, stencilled letters:
"DEFENSE D'AFFLICHER!" and "POST NO BILLS!"

What argues blatantly against itself won't last.
That's sense for everyone as well as Solon.
Whatever law outlives our changing weather
should be less partial, and no occasion
for the proscription of our former friends.

What if our tyrants lied, and someone like them
pastes over what they said? The glassy sidewalk
zebras the black and white tonight under a streetlight.
We owe our tyrants truth, Charlotte. One affirmation
despite Raynal, outlasting Medes and Persians.

"PERPETUAL lying and perpetual murder"–
and thus spake Nietzsche, beyond good and evil.
Prophets proved right and to their own damnation:
morals new stories hide in truth to telling
fictions more pure than history or headlines.

What whispers at our ear is not salvation:
ethics of the occasion, beyond good and evil.
To lie, like Marlow, is to die a little
let in the darkness to the heart, condoning
murder. Interest and profits of our own damnation.

What if our leaders lied, and we believed them?
We owe our tyrants truth. Each small deception
opens the doors and closes off escape.
New rods for old, the keys of charnel houses. . .
Believe the myths–the Furies, not the gods.

CORRUPTION'S what it's all about, Corday.
Our friends are growing older—by decades
in a week—grown slanderous against us.
Our enemies are more consistent:
Danton, that lecherous tun; "Sea Green"

and "Incorruptible" and Cold as Hell
all envy in a Petty Advocate, hell-
bent out of the Provinces to make a name
cost what it will—Robespierre. The Terror
is the fear there'll be men left to judge him.

Brutus served up his sons. This one has
none—but us. Ask any daughter
what it means to have so many corpses
brought, littered, home. Corday, a seed's a meadow.
One lie undoes us all, one slip of tongue.

SORROW to Sorrow, as the sparks fly upward.
Harvard wears white, a scarlet fist, and "Strike!"
The crocuses push up between fruit peelings, litter–
flames out of Pluto's kingdom of the night.
Less eloquent, perhaps, that were the tongues of men.

Will Harvard's Corporation in its Clubs
hear anything of this? The twins turn on the She-Wolf
spew out the little lies and mighty claims.
If what might civilize is used to tyrannize
then test our anger. Every word is suspect

the cries are gutteral, block the radio jam.
Spoilt children, or true rebels? Nothing
will tell but time translated into teaching.
Cold commentary. Old P.R.O.s of Privilege.
We give that privilege back, wear scarlet, white.

SEEK out EMERGENCY, white, hopeless halls
where I wait out the hours with wounded friends
and hear how near the ships are to being burned
while every hero sits and bleeds and fills out forms—
or with your Shield or on it, you'll not pass.

Glass doors blow open on the midnight streets.
The carriage wheels wail rubber as they turn.
Was this the moment—or did it come later?—
when Aphrodite's dummy mimicked their lost wives
and great Odysseus choked the boy and saved our lives?

I am forgetting why I came, while white nepenthe
works through my veins, uproots the cruel pain
others had planted there for secret ends. I rose alone
alone unscathed out of some corner brawl, some reckless wreck—
too late to brake. A stoplight screaming GO!

TODAY, I cruise the Combat Zone
the Copley bar, the Greyhound Station.
One at the last was showing off a knife
to kill his ex-boss, or his wife.
I don't know all the answers. I'm an alien.

Seven were here and seven took their places.
I knew the face of one, a certain spy
who worked in Mantua and gave away
scores of the Carbonari. In the Austrian
pay, he later fought for Garibaldi.

Another was a diver for his living
and hauled up sponges off Kalymnos . . .
died in a brawl suspiciously, although
whether a Royalist or Communist
I neither know nor care. We buried him.

THERE was a brave lie in Rococo
it took an age to see. Artists
aristocrats, who knew that very soon
something was coming to dismay them.
An art of ostriches, perhaps, but who

is stupid—the starers down, the buriers
of heads in sand soon to be severed?
"I need an island in the sun," said Flaubert:
"a tranquil country." "What country?"
writes back George Sand, "against a struggle

that is universal?" Escape then if you can
into the head; in artificial music, manners
Fragonard's gardens, Watteau's island.
Unlike grand, graceless gestures
our laughter has the horror of the end.

WHERE so much silk and lace hides what?—
His smirks and cringes: "*Sol per sfogar il cor*"—
all for our entertainment. Nothing deep
that mercury won't cure. Manners and mask
become the man, like patches on a playful woman.

Don't ask me to dissect or scalpel for a soul
under so many levels. He flatters, panders for
the great. The less-than-great he patronizes.
Dandy and fop and conversationalist and player
in every scene. He'll die too game for laughter

and leave the cut strings dancing on the air, mere
gossamer, and yet how strong, how subtle.
A parasite and poisoner. Bad taste and ranting
genius he foil-flays with his wit. How keen
his envy cuts us. Pretender, murderer of pretense.

CHARLOTTE, I say—"all, all are punishéd!"
By glass that spills the private nightmare on the street.
By glass that leaks the public nightmare on the mind.
Terror for terror. Error echoing error.
Charlotte I say—"all, all are punishéd!"

I stare through windows where the windows show
a cast of naphtha blue. Each flickering screen
repeats last night's repeats, aorist scenes
replay by replay to applause or screams
or bursts of laughter, all relaid on tape.

Watchers and shadows, substitutes and friends
the Tyrant waves, and here one sequence ends.
You pose with Brutus, promise all the names.
A bomber crashes. Canned *Ça Iras* rise.
Then, somewhere in the night, a real child cries.

OUTRAGE is just beginning for the dead.
Naked and racked, dismembered, we'll all lie
to answer questions on no couch or bed—
altar of stone, wet knife, the gutters high.
Nothing we knew in life to this cold mangling.

Forget the doctors, they were hired and paid.
Forget David, he wasn't worth your hate—
fawning and groveling then, as few Court painters.
You were Corday, then wipe away his spit.
He was David, he wasn't worth a shit.

Brood on another altar, owls, a glade
a naked priestess with a moon-shaped blade.
Slow, gurgling Lethe—Drink, there, Charlotte, drink!
The pictured river fades. Mists disappear.
Only a virgin drinking leaves the glass so clear.

CUT with white crosses, framed in shells of gold—
what Simian shadows, what brief clouds they hold.
Tonight, when there's no moon, the white moths fly
against the lamp and find the means to burn.
I turn the pages of a picturebook.

A gypsy woman with a grave and Grecian look
stares at a Punchinello's nose in stone.
Leaning, half naked, over her a youth points out
the figure on the tombslab to two turbaned sages.
A snake curls round a staff. Crouched on a crocodile

a ruffled owl glares at me all the while
the others are engaged. A second woman plays on pipes
but these are silent. On a rock, a bone, an hourglass.
In timeless Arcady what arcane tale's half told?
Cut with white crosses, framed in shells of gold.

CHARLOTTE, perhaps some restless tyrant of the night dictates:
"Beware of country girls, green ribbons in their hair.
"Double the list of spies. Watch all the roads from Caen."
Then sees his secretary's uncontrolled fatigue
take hold on him. The loose head lolls and drops.

—Puppet—perhaps he thinks—I jerk the strings, but what
untwists the rings? I'm tired of taking slack—
Observing his own features in the clock
maybe he thinks—Some more than human force
it took to move the mass of all inert and small

grains that make up the gravity of human fate
that now rolls back on us. At any rate
I'm tired. Where every shadow is a sheath, I wait
the assassin's hour with targets on my chest—
Charlotte, perhaps some restless tyrant of the night . . .

CONFESS, a prisoner in a scarlet dress.
Rain soaks the robe, shows all the woman's form.
Her arms are bound behind. She climbs
a scaffold, has no head, but this may be
a trick of light.

Our wingless Victory of Samothrace
poised on a crag where black Aegean waters race.
Whatever runs like rain across the glass
erases all past images
but this.

Legros lifts up the missing head
swings it above the crowd, then slaps the face.
Blood rushes up. The pale cheeks blush.
But, Charlotte, you were dead.
Were dead.

CORDAY

The historical Marie Anne Charlotte Corday d'Armont was not a Royalist, as I was once led to believe, but, in her own words, "a revolutionary before the revolution." Her family, noble since 1077, had fallen almost to the ranks of the peasants – peasants with pretentions. Her father wrote and spoke against the Court.

Charlotte was born in the village of Ligneries, Normandy, in 1768. The eldest daughter, she became virtually the head of the struggling family in her early teens, her mother sick, her father preoccupied with his writing and his law suits. After the mother's death, the Cordays moved to Caen, where Charlotte attended a Convent school until the suppression of religious institutions. She became the companion to an elderly woman. She was attractive, if not pretty, and managed to avoid being included in the gossip of a provincial town by keeping to herself and reading. She read the classical tragedies of her great-grandfather, Pierre Corneille, and Plutarch's *Lives,* Rousseau and Raynal. From Corneille and Plutarch she drew the idea of "Republican Roman Virtue," which was nothing if not fashionable at the time. From Rousseau came the counter belief in the supremacy of the emotions. She learned from Raynal that it is no crime to lie to illegitimate authority – a theme I argue with here. It is especially interesting, then, that the only moment during her trial when she showed regret for anything she had done was in admitting she was sorry she had used dissimulation to win an entrance into Marat's house. Thus she disowned Raynal's teaching.

In June 1793, the party with which Charlotte Corday allied herself, the moderate Girondists, fell from power. Exiled from the Convention and from Paris, they made their headquarters in Caen. There was a virtual civil war. Paris became the Jacobin center. The Terror and the drawing up of proscription lists had begun. Real power in the purged Convention shifted to Robespierre and Danton – with Marat the most vocal, most feared, and most celebrated of the Jacobin triumvir.

From her encounters with the Girondist leaders in Caen Charlotte must have realized they were largely ineffective, already doomed. At any rate, after considerable anguish she decided to act on her own. She set out for Paris, slept for fifteen hours after her journey at her hotel, then went out to buy a knife – a baker's knife – at a shop in the Rue Royale. Her first attempt to enter Marat's house with the offer of a list of all the leading Girondists in Caen failed. She returned, promised her help once more as a Jacobin informer, and was admitted. She was taken directly to Marat, who was in a medicinal bath because of a chronic skin disease, which, with overwork, was killing him. He wrote on a board across the bath, while printers' assistants waited to rush his copy to the presses. Charlotte Corday stabbed Marat, killing him with one blow of the knife.

She paused, knife in hand, when Marat's common-law wife, Simonne Evrard, rushed in, horrified, to find him dead. Charlotte had had no idea that such a man could be loved. Her hesitation cost her any chance of escape, and she was only saved from being torn apart by the mob through the cool-headedness of one of the arresting police.

Her trial was fairer than most at the time, and is fully documented. It shows that she had a sense of humor, and that her accusers had odd preoccupations. In her pretrial interrogations almost the only questions asked were demands to know who had put her up to the deed – what *men* were her accomplices? After her execution an autopsy was ordered, the sole purpose of which seems to have been to determine whether or not she *was* a virgin. For some reason of their own the fact that she was a virgin proved to those Frenchmen that she had not been lying: she had acted on her own.

The painter Jacques-Louis David is said to have spat on her corpse. This would have been wholly in character with the man Robespierre declared was "born to be a lackey." David was given the task of organizing the apotheosis of Marat, which he accomplished brilliantly, both in an elaborate ceremony (a procession and burial which was a tour-de-force as propaganda) and in his best known painting – Marat as martyr.

The results of Charlotte Corday's action mocked her aims. Her death did not save her party, nor did the death of Marat save anyone on the proscription lists. In execution, they were now offered to the unappeasable shade of the dead "hero." Charlotte Corday became at once the heroine of contemporary poets, many of whom died on the scaffold. As early as 1797 a play was written entitled *"La Judith Moderne."* One wonders if it was ever played, or whether it was read in secret.

Her ambiguous figure still haunts the imagination. She brings out the Partisan in most Frenchmen. She sleepwalks through the *"Marat/Sade"* of Peter Weiss. Over almost two hundred years she has fascinated many; few have been fair to her. In this book she suffers from a number of things, including a sort of Ovidian metamorphosis. But where I argue with her, it is an argument informed by respect – warmed almost by love.

The *Commedia dell'Arte* and Goldoni's plays are often present here; so, on quite different themes, are plays by Corneille. Visual sources that have influenced me are the work of the Tiepolos – the etchings of the *Scherzi di Fantasia* by Giovanni Battista Tiepolo, and the pen and ink punchinello scenes of Giovanni Domenico Tiepolo. It is no accident that there are close to eighty poems here, as there are eighty plates in Goya's *Caprichios.* But perhaps the most personal source – one I have lived with for years – is an engraving of Charlotte Corday, found in an antique shop in Bardstown, Kentucky.

Michael Mott
Williamsburg
May, 1986